P9-DOF-927

The Timucua

EMILY J. DOLBEAR
AND PETER BENOIT

Children's Press®
An Imprint of Scholastic Inc.
New York Toronto London Auckland Sydney
Mexico City New Delhi Hong Kong
Danbury, Connecticut

Content Consultant
Scott Manning Stevens, PhD
Director, McNickle Center
Newberry Library
Chicago, Illinois

Library of Congress Cataloging-in-Publication Data

Dolbear, Emily J.
The Timucua/Emily J. Dolbear and Peter Benoit.
p. cm.—(A true book)
Includes bibliographical references and index.
ISBN-13: 978-0-531-20767-3 (lib. bdg.) 978-0-531-29309-6 (pbk.)
ISBN-10: 0-531-20767-6 (lib. bdg.) 0-531-29309-2 (pbk.)
1. Timucua Indians—Juvenile literature. I. Benoit, Peter, 1955– II. Title. III. Series.
E99.T55D65 2011
975.9'01—dc22 2010049077

Printed in China 62

2 3 4 5 6 7 8 9 10 R 19 18 17 16 15 14 13 12

Find the Truth!

Everything you are about to read is true ***except*** for one of the sentences on this page.

Which one is **TRUE**?

T or F Today, there are no living Timucua Indians.

T or F The language of the Timucua Indians is related to Spanish.

Find the answers in this book.

Contents

Timucua warrior and child

The Timucua grew large fields of pumpkins and other crops.

The hair of many Timucua women was long enough to reach their hips.

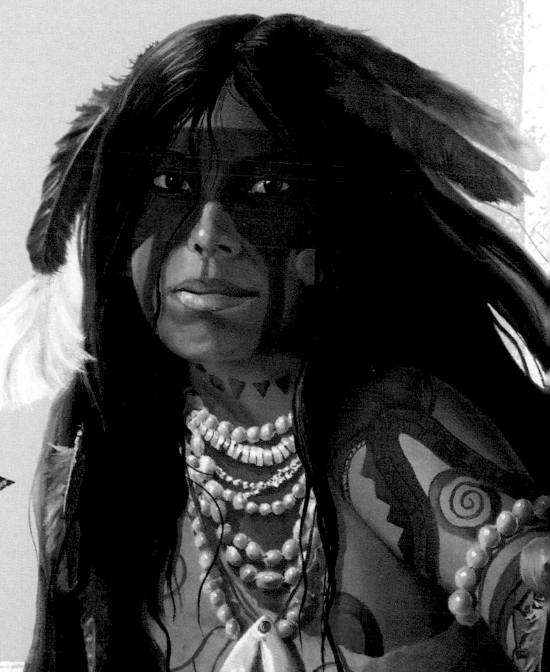

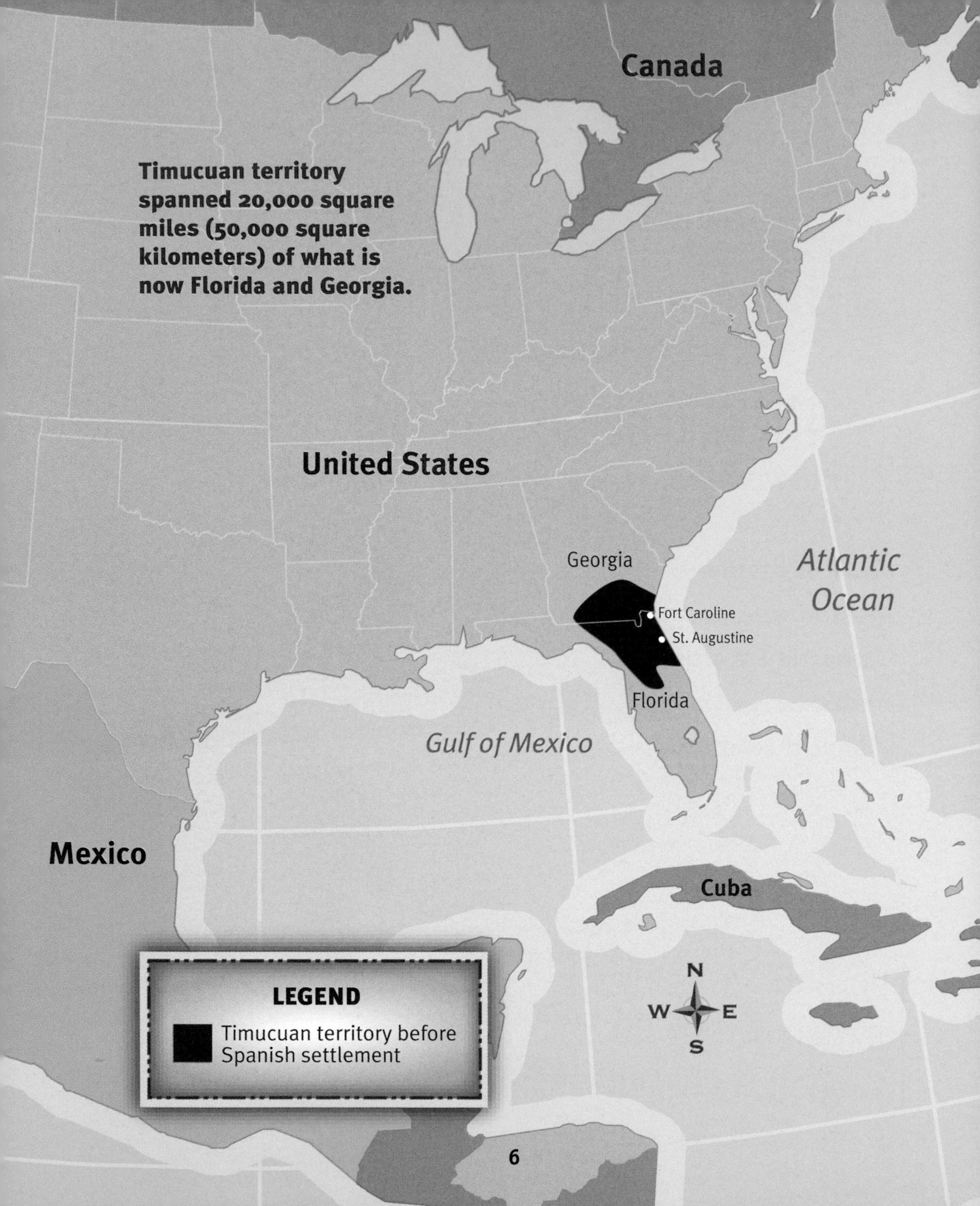
Canada
Timucuan territory spanned 20,000 square miles (50,000 square kilometers) of what is now Florida and Georgia.
United States
Georgia
Fort Caroline
St. Augustine
Atlantic Ocean
Florida
Gulf of Mexico
Mexico
Cuba
LEGEND
Timucuan territory before Spanish settlement
N
W
E
S

La Florida

By the time the area now called Florida got its name, Native Americans had been living in the region for thousands of years. The Timucua (tee-MOO-kwa) were some of the earliest known people in the area. They hunted, fished, and farmed in today's north-central Florida and southeast Georgia. Their Native American neighbors included the Apalachee to the northwest, the Calusa to the southwest, and the Tequesta along the southeastern coast.

The Timucua were once the largest Native American group in the area.

A Land in Full Bloom

Juan Ponce de León

Jump back into the sixteenth century. Spanish explorer Juan Ponce de León and his crew had been at sea for a month. In early April 1513, he spotted land from his ship.

The next day, the Spanish sailors came ashore, probably near the modern-day city of Saint Augustine, Florida. They wanted to explore and claim the land for Spain.

Ponce de León gave this land the name *La Florida*. That means "land of flowers" in Spanish.

Ponce de León was the first explorer to claim part of the North American mainland for Spain.

Ponce de León's crew explores Florida. At first, Ponce de León thought he had reached an island.

The Spanish explorers found more than just a land in full bloom. People they had never seen before were there, too—the Timucua. Native Americans lived comfortably in La Florida before the arrival of the Europeans. They numbered between 200,000 and 900,000. But about 250 years after Ponce de León landed, the Timucua were completely gone.

In 1539, de Soto landed at what is now Tampa Bay, Florida.

CHAPTER 2

European Settlement

Ponce de León's 1513 **expedition** was the first of many European efforts to **colonize** La Florida. Another Spanish explorer named Hernando de Soto led a small army through northern Florida in 1539. They killed hundreds of Timucua in their quest for riches. De Soto never found gold, and he died of fever in 1542.

Once ashore, de Soto claimed to be a sun god in an effort to impress the Timucua.

The Spanish Against the French

By 1564, the French had built a settlement along the Saint Johns River in La Florida. Fort Caroline was the first French colony in today's United States.

But King Philip II of Spain wanted La Florida for himself. He sent Pedro Menéndez de Avilés (PED-roh meh-NEN-dehz DEH ah-vee-LEZ) to take back the land. In 1565, Menéndez and more than 500 soldiers set up camp in the Timucua village called Seloy. During a driving rainstorm, they attacked the French settlers and took Fort Caroline. Spain now had control of La Florida and its people.

A French soldier with two Timucua. The French traded goods such as combs to the Timucua for food.

Drawing the Timucua

Jacques Le Moyne was the first European artist in North America. He was a member of the French expedition to La Florida that built Fort Caroline in 1564. In his detailed drawings, he captured the Timucua ways of life. He showed the Timucua chasing deer, hunting alligators, paddling canoes, and swimming. Years later, these illustrations were turned into **engravings** by a Flemish **goldsmith** named Theodor de Bry.

This de Bry engraving shows Timucua men hunting deer. Hidden under deerskins, they were able to get close to the animals without scaring them.

Setting Up Missions

To establish power over this new land, the Spanish began setting up **missions**. Missions were villages built to settle the land and **convert** Native Americans to Christianity. The missions were run by friars. Friars are members of a religious community who teach and preach.

The missions were not only used to spread Christianity. They were also a way to make Native Americans more like the Spanish. The Timucua had to learn Spanish. Timucua at the missions were also a source of labor for the Spanish.

A friar oversees the burial of a Timucua at a Florida mission.

Today, a shrine is located at the Mission Nombre de Dios site.

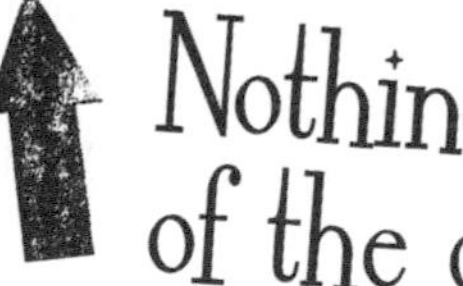

Nothing remains today of the original mission.

The First Spanish Mission

The Spanish forced Timucua Indians to help build the mission of Saint Augustine in 1565. They called it Mission Nombre de Dios (NOME-bray DEH DEE-oss), which means "name of God" in Spanish. It was the first Spanish mission in what we now call the United States.

CATECISMO
EN LENGVA
TIMVQVANA, Y CASTELLANA,
en el qual ſe inſtruyen y cathequizan los
adultos infieles que an de ſer Chriſtianos. Y no ſerà menos vtil para
los ya Chriſtianos.

¶ Compueſto por el P. F. Franciſco Pareja, Religio-
ſo de la Orden de N. Seraphico P. S. Franciſco, y Padre
de la Prouincia de Santa Elena de la Florida, natural
de Auñon dioceſi del Arçobiſpado de Toledo.

Año 1627.

¶ CON PRIVILEGIO.
En Mexico, en la Imprenta de Iuan Ruyz.

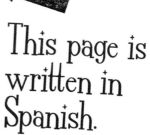

This book of religious writings contains text in both Spanish and Timucua.

This page is written in Spanish.

A Priest With a Mission

In 1595, a mission priest named Francisco Pareja traveled to east Florida's villages to work with the Timucua. He served at the mission of San Juan del Puerto located at the mouth of Saint Johns River. Father Pareja took on the task of translating Spanish religious writings into the Timucua language in 1612. His work became very valuable to the study of Native American history.

Timucua Language

This Timucua chief is from the northeast Florida region. The Timucua language had several words that meant "chief."

The Timucua people had a single language. But they spoke several different forms of the language, or **dialects**. Timucua from different areas used different grammar and words. They even pronounced words differently. Different dialects sometimes meant a lack of unity among the tribal groups. The Timucua were both one people and many peoples.

THE BIG TRUTH!

A Language of the Past

The Timucua language was thousands of years old when the European colonists arrived in the early 1500s. It is a complex language. Timucua is related to no other known languages in the world. The Timucua Indians had no written language. Spanish **missionaries**, including Father Francisco Pareja, helped preserve many Timucua words and phrases. Without the work of these missionaries, no record of this language would exist. It is not clear how to pronounce the words, however. It seems that many words of three or fewer syllables emphasize the first syllable.

Here's a short list of basic Timucuan words:

English	Timucuan	
one	yaha	
two	yucha	
sun	ela	
moon	acu	

Today, researchers are working on a complete word index of the Timucua language.

Inflated fish bladders like the ones worn by this chief were special Timucua ear ornaments.

A Timucua chief

CHAPTER 3

Timucua Ways of Life

There were two major groups of Timucua. The eastern Timucua fished along the Atlantic coast. The western Timucua hunted and built their huts in the forestland of today's northwestern Florida.

The Timucua did not have a single central leader. Instead, they were organized into about thirty-five **chiefdoms**. A chiefdom was the people or territory ruled by a tribal chief. Most chiefdoms had several thousand Timucua scattered over a handful of villages. Each chiefdom usually had one central village.

Timucua Villages

A typical Timucua village contained a few hundred people with perhaps 30 houses. Houses were small and circular. They were usually no larger than 20 feet (6 meters) wide. They might be 70 feet (20 m) apart. Villagers used them mostly for sleeping. Cooking took place in the village, where meals were served daily in a central place.

Timucua traveled in large canoes dug out of a single tree.

Some Timucua villages had as many as 200 houses.

This image shows a reconstruction of what a Timucua house may have looked like.

Houses and Clans

The Timucua drove poles into the ground to build their simple houses. They covered the structures with palm leaves from nearby forests. Walls were woven vines. Clay filled the holes. Smoke escaped from an opening in the top of the house.

The settlement also had a council house where large gatherings were held. The largest villages might have hundreds of members. Each village was divided into family **clans** with animal names. Children belonged to their mother's clan.

Appearance

The Timucua had dark brown skin and long black hair. The men were tall and wore their hair pulled up on their heads. The Timucua dressed in animal skins and woven cloth and moss.

Jewelry was important to the Timucua. Women often wore pearls or beads around their necks, ankles, or elbows.

Skin Decoration

Many Timucua decorated their skin with tattoos. Each tattoo had a special meaning. Tattoos could be a sign of a person's standing in the community as well as individuality. Even children got tattoos as they took on more responsibilities in daily life. To make tattoos, the Timucua made holes in the skin and rubbed ashes in the holes.

Timucua tattoos showed many designs but never featured images of people.

Red, blue, or black were common tattoo colors.

Hunting

Timucua men were skilled hunters. They used spears, clubs, and bows and arrows to kill wild animals. They ate animals such as rabbit, turkey, deer, and bear. They also caught alligators and large sea animals called manatees. They cooked the meat over an open fire.

Women cleaned, made clothing, and prepared food. They cooked broths using meat and nuts that they gathered.

A Timucua boy in the arms of his warrior father holds a bow. Skilled hunters and warriors were important to the Timucua.

Fishing

The Timucua were clever at fishing. They built wood fences called **weirs** (WEERZ) across streams and rivers to trap fish, clams, and oysters. Fish swam over the weir at high tide and were caught when the tide went out.

Men sometimes held arrows in the knot of their hair.

A Timucua fisher examines an arrow. Some fish were caught using bows and arrows.

Twice a year, the Timucua grew crops such as pumpkins.

Farming and Food

The Timucua also farmed. They grew maize (corn), melons, beans, and squash. They ground corn into a powder for use in corn cakes and other dishes. The women collected wild fruits, palm berries, acorns and other nuts, and roots. They baked bread made from the root *koonti*. The women made fine pottery for cooking.

Preparing the Land

Before tilling, Timucua workers cleared the fields of weeds and brush by setting them on fire. They used simple hoes to till the soil and prepare it for planting. Women planted the seeds. Later, they would develop the *coa*, a tool using two sticks, for planting.

The Timucua stored extra crops to be shared later during tougher times.

A group of Timucua transport food that will be stored.

Le Moyne described a Timucua ceremony in which a deer was sacrificed and prayers were offered to the sun in the hope that the land would be productive.

Beliefs

The Timucua believed that different parts of nature were guided by spirits. For example, the sun, the moon, and different animals each had spirits that guided them. Village leaders led prayers and shared a ceremonial porridge before planting new fields. People whistled to help calm rough waters or put an end to storms. Fishers prayed to lake spirits to make certain there would be a good catch for the tribe. They placed caught fish on a smoking rack as an offering.

Timucua Games

The Timucua played many different sports. They were serious about them all. According to European settlers, the Timucua played a game using their feet to shoot a ball against a goalpost. Teams of many players kicked a small ball of dried mud wrapped in buckskin. Another game involved throwing a ball at a target on a post. The winner was the person who hit the target first.

Experts believe that Timucua games were versions of those played by other American Indians to the west and north.

If a Timucua man died, his widow cut her hair short and did not remarry until it grew out.

A widow is shown here scattering her cut hair.

Ceremonies for the Dead

The Timucua held many special ceremonies. When someone died, for example, the Timucua built a mound of sand or oyster shells over the body. They buried the person with meaningful items such as pieces of pottery or arrowheads. The Timucua stopped building burial mounds after the Spanish settlers arrived. The missionaries did not approve of these ceremonies. They pressed the Timucua to bury their dead according to the Catholic religion.

Celebrating

The Timucua celebrated planting, harvesting, and fishing and hunting trips with ceremonies. There were also ceremonies before warfare with other tribes.

Ceremonies might involve feasting or fasting. When people fast, they go without food. Members might pray or dance at important events. The most important members of the tribe led all of these large ceremonies.

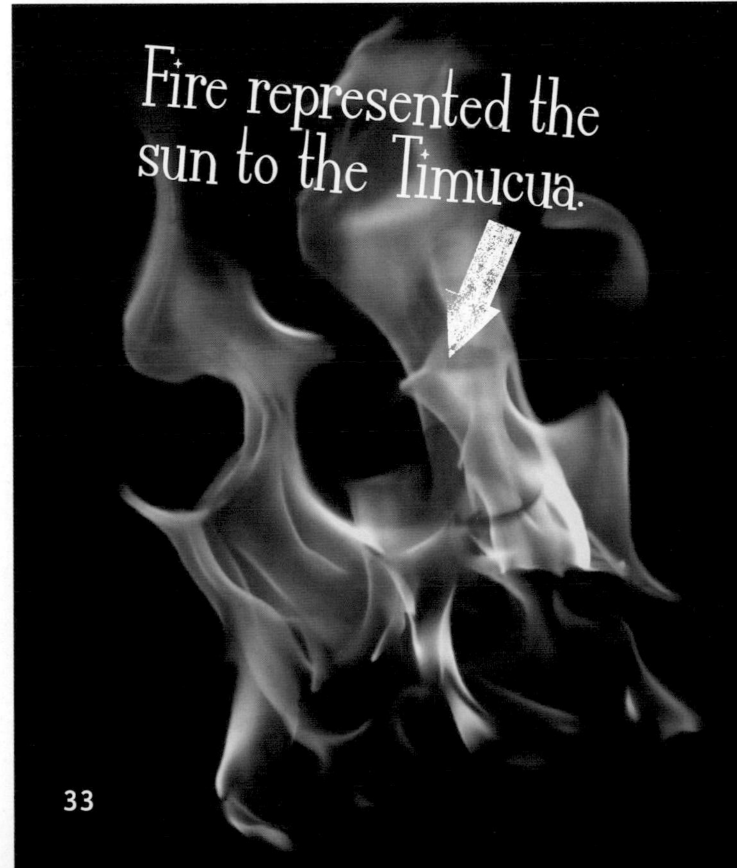
Fire represented the sun to the Timucua.

Lighting a fire was a feature of many Timucua ceremonies.

A Strong Tea

During ceremonies, the Timucua often drank a strong tea called *cassina*. The Timucua made it from the evergreen holly called yaupon (YEW-pahn). They roasted the leaves and brewed them in a large pot of water. Then, they poured the tea into a cup made from the shell of a large sea snail called a lightning whelk.

Some groups traded yaupon leaves for other goods.

Yaupon holly

A warrior vomits after drinking cassina.

The black drink brewed by the Timucua contained a lot of caffeine.

Taking the Black Drink

This ceremonial drink was an important part of the daily meetings of village councils. All male tribal members in good standing were given the dark tea. It often made them sweat and vomit. They believed that this got rid of any sickness in their bodies. After the chief was served, the others drank. Men of lower rank, women, and children were not allowed to touch "the black drink."

At one point, most western Timucua lived in 11 missions.

The End of the Timucua

The Spanish mission system in La Florida grew between 1595 and 1620. Spanish missionaries spread their religion and taught the local people their customs. They introduced the Timucua to their foods. The Native Americans had never seen figs, hazelnuts, or garbanzo beans. Oranges, peaches, and watermelon were also new to the Timucua. They learned how to grow these crops and raise pigs and chickens.

In the early 1700s, Mission Nombre de Dios was called the "village of Timucua."

Forced to Work

At the same time, the Spanish colonists forced more and more of the Timucua to work for them. Timucua built villages and roads. They labored in the fields. They worked as house servants. They even served in Spanish armies, all with little or no pay.

A Timucua farmer works the land. The Spanish came to depend on the Timucua to raise crops. The artist of this image mistakenly shows the man using a European-style farming tool.

Le Moyne described a Timucua treatment for illness in which a person would lie facedown and inhale smoke.

Smallpox killed more than half of the Timucua over a period of four years.

Diseases

Over time, many Timucua Indians died from **infectious** diseases brought by the Europeans. They suffered from smallpox, measles, and yellow fever. The Timucua were losing their people and their culture.

Fighting Back

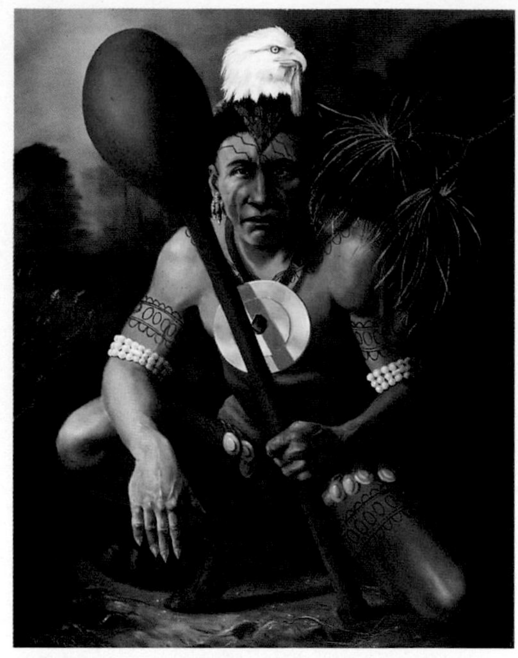

Notice this Timucua war chief's sharp fingernails. Warriors filed their nails to points for use in battle.

In 1656, some Timucua chiefs decided to challenge the orders of the Spanish rulers. They fought back against the Spanish soldiers. The Timucua did not target any of the priests living at the missions. The Spanish overpowered the Timucua in the end. The loss was a great blow to the Timucua leaders.

Timucua Timeline

1513

Juan Ponce de León lands in today's Florida and claims it for Spain.

1565

Spain destroys a French settlement in Florida and forces the Timucua to help build its first mission at Saint Augustine.

Spanish Departure

The Seminole (pictured here) came to Florida in the 18th century and lived south of the Timucua.

In 1763, Britain gained control of Florida from Spain. By then, the Timucua had almost all died out. Some Timucua went to Cuba with Spanish colonists. Others were absorbed into the population of the Seminole who themselves were made up of the Creek and others.

1656 → **1763**

The Timucua rebel against the Spanish.

By the time Spain gives up Florida land to the British, the Timucua people have mostly died out.

A People No More

Disease, clashes with colonists, forced labor, and finally raids by other tribes and English slave traders had destroyed this tribe in about 250 years. Burial mounds, pottery remains, and pages of Timucua text written by Spanish missionaries are all that remain. ★

Creating accurate images of a people that no longer exists takes a lot of study and attention to detail.

True Statistics

Number of soldiers Pedro Menéndez de Avilés brought to take back La Florida: More than 500

Year Mission Nombre de Dios was founded: 1565

Estimated number of Timucua chiefdoms: 35

Number of Native Americans living in La Florida in early 1500s: Between 200,000 and 900,000

Number of Timucua Indians today: 0

Number of years between the arrival of Europeans and the end of the Timucua: About 250

Did you find the truth?

T Today, there are no living Timucua Indians.

F The language of the Timucua Indians is related to Spanish.

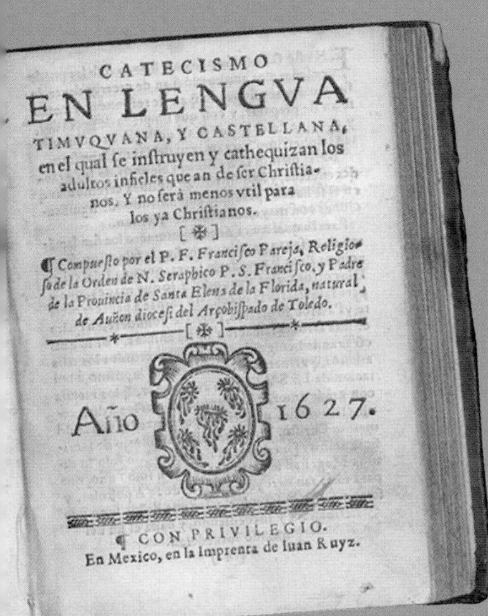

CATECISMO
EN LENGVA
TIMVQVANA, Y CASTELLANA,
en el qual se instruyen y cathequizan los
adultos infieles que an de ser Christianos. Y no será menos vtil para
los ya Christianos.

¶ Compuesto por el P. F. Francisco Pareja, Religio-
so de la Orden de N. Seraphico P. S. Francisco, y Padre
de la Prouincia de Santa Elena de la Florida, natural
de Auñon diocesi del Arçobispado de Toledo.

Año 1627.

¶ CON PRIVILEGIO.
En Mexico, en la Imprenta de Iuan Ruyz.

A Spanish book of religious writings

Resources

Books

Dennis, Yvonne Wakim, and Arlene Hirschfelder. *A Kid's Guide to Native American History: More Than 50 Activities*. Chicago: Chicago Review Press, 2010.

Gioia, Robyn. *America's First Real Thanksgiving: St. Augustine, Florida, September 8, 1565*. Sarasota, FL: Pineapple Press, 2006.

Mountjoy, Shane. *St. Augustine*. New York: Chelsea House, 2007.

Perritano, John. *Spanish Missions*. New York: Children's Press, 2010.

Petrie, Kristin. *Juan Ponce de León*. Edina, MN: Abdo, 2007.

Somervill, Barbara. *Florida*. New York: Children's Press, 2008.

Suben, Eric. *The Spanish Missions of Florida*. New York: Children's Press, 2010.

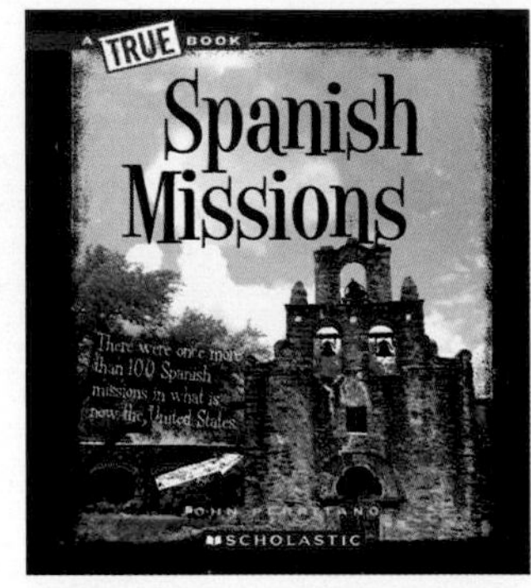

Organizations and Web Sites

Ancient Native—Heritage of the Ancient Ones: Vocabulary List of Timucuan Words
www.ancientnative.org/voc.php
Learn more about the Timucua language.

Timucuan Trail State and National Parks
www.timucuantrail.com
Find out more about the natural beauty and rich history of the Timucuan Trail State and National Parks.

Places to Visit

Timucuan Ecological and Historic National Preserve
12713 Fort Caroline Road
Jacksonville, FL 32225
(904) 641-7155
www.nps.gov/timu
Discover 6,000 years of human history.

Tomoka State Park
2099 North Beach Street
Ormond Beach, FL 32174
(386) 676-4050
www.floridastateparks.org/tomoka
Walk the historic trail that passes through the ancient Timucua village site of Nocoroco.

Important Words

chiefdoms (CHEEF-duhmz)—the peoples or territories over which a single chief rules

clans (KLANZ)—social groups that are smaller than a tribe and larger than a family

colonize (KOL-uh-nize)—to start a colony, which is an area ruled by another country

convert (kuhn-VURT)—to change someone's beliefs

dialects (DYE-uh-lektss)—different forms of a single language

engravings (en-GRAY-vinghz)—images printed from carved blocks

expedition (ek-spuh-DISH-uhn)—a journey taken for a specific purpose

goldsmith (GOHLD-smith)—a person who makes items out of gold or trades them

infectious (in-FEK-shuhss)—capable of spreading from one person to another

missionaries (MISH-uh-ner-eez)—people who try to spread their religious beliefs to others

missions (MISH-uhnz)—villages built to settle the land and convert the local people

weirs (WEERZ)—wood fences placed in a stream to catch fish

Index

Page numbers in **bold** indicate illustrations

About the Authors

Emily J. Dolbear works as a freelance editor and writer of children's books. Dolbear lives with her family in Brookline, Massachusetts.

Peter Benoit is educated as a mathematician but has many other interests. He has taught and tutored high school and college students for many years, mostly in math and science. He also runs summer workshops for writers and students of literature. Benoit has written more than 2,000 poems. His life has been one committed to learning. He lives in Greenwich, New York.

PHOTOGRAPHS© 2011: Alamy Images: 15 (America), 41 top (North Wind Picture Archives); Clifford Oliver Photography/www.cliffordoliverphotography.com: 48 bottom; Fountain of Youth Archaeological Park, St. Augustine, FL/Hollis Holbrook: 14; Grant Heilman Photography, Inc: 34; iStockphoto/Tan Kian Khoon: 33; Library of Congress: 38 (Theodor de Bry), back cover, 16, 43 (Jay I. Kislak Collection); Mary E. Dolbear: 48 top; National Park Service, Timucuan Ecological & Historic Preserve/Richard Schlecht: 3, 12, 22; North Wind Picture Archives: 9; Scholastic Library Publishing, Inc.: 44; ShutterStock, Inc.: 5 top, 28 (Don Bendickson), 18, 19 (Workmans Photos); Courtesy of the St. Augustine Foundation, Inc., Flagler College: 23; Courtesy of the State Archives of Florida/Stanley Meltzoff: 36; The Design Lab: 6; The Granger Collection, New York: 13, 29, 30, 31 (Theodor de Bry), 8, 10, 40 bottom; Theodore Morris/www.floridalosttribes.com: cover, 4, 5 bottom, 17, 20, 24, 25, 26, 27, 40 top, 42; University of South Florida/The Florida Center for Instructional Technology: 32, 35, 39, 41 bottom.